RiverSpeak

Other Books by Greg Nielsen

MetaBusiness: Creating a New Global Culture

Tuning to the Spiritual Frequencies

Beyond Pendulum Power

Pendulum Power

Pyramid Power

RiverSpeak

Greg Nielsen

Conscious Books

Reno, Nevada
USA

RiverSpeak

By Greg Nielsen

Conscious Books
316 California Ave., Suite 210
Reno, Nevada 89509
800-322-9943

e-mail: greg.nielsen@charter.net
website: www.gregnielsen.net

First Quality Paperback Book Edition 2006

10 9 8 7 6 5 4 3 2 1

Library of Congress
Card Catalog Number: 2006902117

ISBN 0-9619917-4-7

Printed and Bound in The United States of America

Cover art by Cyndee Chavez – bcreativedesign@mac.com

Cover and book design by White Sage Studios
Virginia City, Nevada – whitesage@gbis.com

Author photo: © Ronda Chatelle – rchatelle@comcast.net

RiverSpeak

1

RiverSpeak

Ripples of white water bubble
Telling the story of light and dark.
The message is clear and simple
Your language is RiverSpeak.

Over and over you ripple and bubble,
White water back to mysterious shade of rock.
The sun's rays are quiet there.
The current travels passed
Fish and microscopic creatures.

RiverSpeak sends a message from
Snowy mountaintops to ocean body
Or great lake.
Long distance at the speed of water,
As above, so below.
Aqua Divinum coursing through the soul,
Ripple, bubble, splash.

2

Bend in the River

Tell me about bending;
You're never straight and narrow.
Always bending, turning, churning,
Your curves are well rounded.

"We bend because we feel beautiful.
When you look at us your eyes
Scan our curves.
Your vision relaxes through the bend.

We have more fun when we take a turn,
Sometimes for the worse,
Sometimes for the better.
We surprise you and ourselves.
We're never bored because we bend."

3

Riding the Current

Whatever floats river carries,
Leaf, twig, feather.
Muscular currents,
Eddies flexing,
Ripples swirling.

Counting the small things
Riding the current downstream.
Can't count them fast enough.
If you were to gather them
All together
It would take a convoy of dump trucks
To haul them to river's end.

River carries them with ease,
Going with the flow.
You hardly notice them,
Floating by
Riding the current downstream.

4

Where the Water Falls

Plunging water applauds.
White water on stage,
Dancing from rock to rock.

River is most alive at the falls,
Raw water,
A force to reckon with.
You can feel the coolness,
Even on the hottest summer day.

You walk away exhilarated,
Your soul energized
With essence of river.
You feel river inside
Your body.

5

After a Rain

After a Rain,
River rushes, swells, rises.
Urgency, work to be done.
It can't be put off
Until tomorrow.

Rain joins river,
Giving life.
Invigorated,
Rain is eager
To see its new home
Downstream.

River shows the way.
Reaching the sea,
Rain guides river
Toward the sky.
Eventually, river becomes rain.

6

River Giggles

River quiet,
River roar.
River fast,
River slow.

River splish, splash
Like a child.
Then turns into a monster,
Devouring.
Hungry for rocks and trees,
Bridges and cars.

After the flood,
River giggles innocently
Through the rapids
And is silent.

Along flat stretches,
Napping under the warm
Indian summer sun.

7

Refuge in the River

I come to river to listen.
There are no words
Yet I hear a message
In my heart.

A gaggle of geese
Lands in front of me,
A symphonic splash
In the sun speckled current.

Honking, they settle down,
Resting after a long flight.
I hear thoughts,
'Take refuge in the river,
Rest up for the next
Leg of the journey.
Bathe, drink, swim, play,
Soon you will take flight again.'

8

The River Roars

Car traffic,
The drone of machines;
I can barely hear
The river passing
Under a bridge.
I concentrate, listening
To RiverSpeak.

The machines roar
They interrupt
I keep listening;
I don't stop listening,
No matter the drone and roar.

I move closer;
I hear water calling,
Falling from one level
To another.

Where water falls
There's energy,
A natural resonance,
Revitalizing.
The motors are quiet now;
The river roars.

9

River Ever Falling

River alive
With motion.
Gravity moving
River downstream.

River is always falling,
Never afraid
Of falling.
Since earth holds
River in its arms
As it falls,
Plunging toward the sea.

10

Riverscape

Sunshine dances on
Rippling waters,
Wavelets of light and shade.

On the riverbank
Foliage yellow, red and orange.
Through the falling leaves
Light blinds.

Unless you're in the sun
The cool fall air sends
A shiver through you.

Watching the rushing water,
You feel movement within,
Energy revitalizing the blood.

Your heart beats
To the rhythm of the ripples.
Dancing water
Plays in your heart.
There's more than meets
The eye.

11

Sitting by the River

I just like sitting by the river;
It has a smell that clears my head.
I feel more peaceful;
Time slows down.

The rush goes away.
My ears open to river's sounds.
The tensions flow
Out of my body, downstream.

River was here before me;
It will be here after me.
I'm not so important
When sitting by the river.

River doesn't fight gravity
Like I do.
I get all caught up.
River is just river.

Water flowing, ever wet
Always bending to earth's resistance.
Sitting by the river,
I like it;
I feel better.

12

River Teach

River teaches
Everything you need to know.
When I touch river
The cool water touches me.
River cools you off when you're hot.

When I look at river
I see it always moving.
Slowly in some places,
Faster in others.

When you resist the flow
You're like a big rock
In the river.
The flowing water
Sculpts and smoothes
The edges at first.
But eventually, over time,
The rock is carved away.
Only grains of sand are left.

13
River's Razor Edge

Winter has clutched river;
The waters are chilled bone.
Black-grey skies penetrate
The moving waters with dark shades.

North winds tear brown leaves
From barren branches.
A flotilla of dead leaves
Ride the currents.

River is less inviting now;
Fewer people are drawn
To river's razor edge.
Once in awhile I see
A fisherman casting.
He loves to fish;
He loves the river's solitude,
The cold bone waters
And the black-grey skies.
They can't keep him
From river's razor edge.

14

Dressed in Grey

River dressed in shades
Of day and night,
Upstream and down.
The fashion never changes,
Yet the waters ever
Rise and fall around
Boulder-bone and rock-skin.

River is most attractive
Wearing a jeweled crown
And a flowing dress
Of grey granite,
Grey bark and grey clouds.

To keep warm
River wraps itself
In a brown shawl.
River forever wades
Never getting cold feet,
Even in winter.

15

Back to River

The rushing water invigorates,
Even more after being
Away so long.
It's been more than
Two months
Since embracing the river.

It's a sunny day
In February
And the winds are calm.
I've found a new secret spot
Beside the river,
Like no one has sat
Here before.

The winter sun
On cold snow melted waters.
The tree branches stretch
Toward the ice blue sky.
I feel the cascading river
Rushing through my body.
I'm invigorated;
It's good to be back.

16

River Watching

Sitting on a granite slab
Beside the river
Watching the effervescent
Ever present flow.
The morning sun creates
White, green, brown,
Black and blue waters.

The granite slab
I'm sitting on
Is worn smooth
By the river.
River smoothes out
The rough edges,
Rounds out the angles,
Polishes the dull surfaces.

Watching the river,
I see the curves
In the corner,
The fire in the water
And the softness
In the granite slab
I'm sitting on.

17

Born in the Sky

Curves and turns,
Undulating toward the sea.
Born in the sky,
In the mountains high.
Sees all, knows all,
Lives where we all live.
Highlands, lowlands,
Peaks, valleys,
Wetlands, desert
And beach.

Hundreds, thousands,
Tens of thousands
Of years.
Turning, curving,
Undulating toward the sea.
River stretches
Across the landscape.
To river there's no such thing
As the shortest distance
Between two points.

18

Truly a Poet

River says it all
Without ever uttering
A word.
The rhythm and rhyme,
Nature's poetry in motion,
Wordless expression,
Silent inspiration.

RiverSpeak,
A universal language
Experienced by anyone,
Anywhere, any time.
No need for an alphabet,
Vowels and consonances.

River's wordless writing,
The poetry
That poets read
And listen to.
The poet of poets,
River is truly a poet.

19

Spring Announcement

Swift current,
Rushing water,
Dancing sunlight.
Ripples and eddies,
River rock smooth.
Snow melting,
Spring time,
Warm sun.
River's edge,
Bird's bathing,
Drinking, playing.
River people sitting,
Enjoying rushing water,
Dancing sunlight.
Spring by the river,
In the river.

20
The Heart of the City

River, the city's blood.
The pressure, the pulse, the beat.
Blood pumping through
The heart of the city.
Under bridges, next to buildings,
River carries life.
Blood sustains the city's citizens.
Without it they would die.
Remember the drought years,
Every drop was precious.
River was reduced to a trickle.
We wondered,
'Will there be enough
To go around?'
Watering the lawns
Wasn't so important.
Feel your heart beat
In sync with the river.
City's blood, your blood.
The heart of the city.

21

River's Call

I've been working all day
In a busy office.
The phone rings incessantly
To the point where
I don't want to answer.
My thoughts go to river.
I hear the rushing rapids;
I answer the call.

Leaving the workplace,
I make my way
To the river
Just a few blocks away.
Sitting quietly, I listen
To the river sounds,
Natural music.

I feel it flowing through me.
The busy office and frazzled rings
Are swept downstream.
I'm glad I answered
River's call.

22

River On My Mind

River on my mind;
My thoughts are fluid,
My thoughts are lucid.
Thinking of nothing in particular,
Hearing river flowing behind me
River on my mind.

Resisting the urge to turn around
And look at river,
I see river in my mind,
Picture perfect undulating flow,
Bumpy currents, white water.

Ever-present cool boil,
Evaporating serpentine coil
The rivers of my mind.
Feeling the regeneration,
Enjoying the rejuvenation,
Riding current imagination.
The world between worlds,
River on my mind.

23
Fork in the River

A fork in the river,
Converges and merges.
An upper and a lower,
A north fork and a south.
Two journeys, two paths;
One river, divided
Coming together as one.
Two experiences shared.

What does river have to say?
"Rather than cut a direct path,
It's easier to divide,
Leaving the earth alone
To grow its trees and flowers.
Besides, by bending
We experience so much more.
Converging we have
So much to share."

24

Mind Ride

My mind rides river,
Wild, winding and windy.
Raw energy, water force
Tumbling head over heels
From snowcaps to whitecaps,
Spraying and splashing,
Surging from bank to bank,
From glacier to seascape.

My mind is acute,
Eddies and swirls,
Timeful capsules, thought currents,
Bubbling whitewater shapes
Alive all around me.

River thinks clearly
At all times.
Mind without illusion,
Mind without confusion.

25

Invisible Geysers

A green spectrum,
Spring beside and around river.
Bright greens,
Full of sunshine.
River feeds the trees,
Grasses and shrubs.
Mountain mineral water,
Fresh, cool melted,
Bubbling with vitality.

The roots drink deeply
Of pure water force.
River rises like invisible geysers
Up the trunks
Through the branches
Into the green sunlight.
The leaves dance
Drunk with sweet river.
Whatever is left over
Evaporates into thin air,
Then we inhale river.

26

Drinking Hot Green Tea

A cloudy Sunday morning,
Spring time beside the river.
A cool breeze chills;
I shiver as I drink
Hot green tea.

Heavy weather blows
In from the west.
A kayaker floats by
Smiling, paddling,
Energized by the ride.

River appears agitated;
The current is bumpy,
Turbulent waters churn,
Reflecting heavy, dark
Grey clouds drifting east.
Occasional breaks
In the thick cloud cover
Transforms the river
Into a short-lived
Dance of light.
It takes away the chill
And warms the shiver
As I sip tepid tea.

27

Kaleidoscopic River

Kaleidoscopic river,
Geometric shape shifting waters,
Vibrant run off speeding,
Through the city.
There's nothing meandering
Or gentle in the river now.

Sunny, blue skies
Bring out river's colors,
White, green, gold, brown,
Blue, red, yellow.
Nature's kaleidoscope,
Rivaled only by
The trees in fall.

Perpetually intermingling
Concentric circles and triangles
Peaking and valleying
To the sounds
Of water falling,
Improvisational river jazz.

28

Standing Ovation

Listening to the spring river runoff
It sounds like a continuous
Standing ovation.
The winter performance
Was outstanding;
The actors were superb.
Snow was cold, wet and white
Melting in the final act.

Sun played it low key
Warming earth just a touch.
Throughout the play,
Tree stood leafless
Waiting in the wings
Until the very end
Then burst upon the scene,
Budding and bowing
Even after the curtain call.

River gets up out of its
Comfortable seat and applauds
Another great performance:
Winter starring Sun.

29

White Shimmering

There's something different
In the river
The last few days.
The water is lighter,
Brighter, whiter.
Maybe it has something to do
With the snows melting
In the ninety degree heat.

Usually when the sun
Shines on the moving water
There's a golden glow.
Now there's a white shimmering.

Last night when I fell asleep
I felt the river calling;
The river goddess
Sent me a dream message.
I felt content
Hearing the feeling.
It wasn't words;
It was a knowing that river
Was willing to share its wisdom.
A golden glow,
A white shimmering.

30

River Boulder

Golden brown boulder
Standing firm in the rushing waters,
Soaking in the warm morning sun.
A study in contrast, side by side:

Standing – Running
Solid – Liquid
Form – Formless
Unchanging – Every Changing
Resisting – Unresisting
Earth – Water
Opaque – Transparent
Heavy – Light
Silent – Loud
Peaceful – Turbulent
Rigid – Flexible
Boulder – River

Grain by grain, river
Gnaws away at boulder.
After a millennium,
Boulder will have nothing
To stand on
Dissolving in the rushing waters.

31

Golden Boulder

Sitting on a golden boulder
Along the river bank
I feel a warm wind
Massaging my face.
Hundreds of birds sing
In the trees and underbrush,
Greeting the morning sun.

I'm writing, listening
For RiverSpeak.
The current is stronger
Than usual, unforgiving.
Whatever falls into its grasp
Will be hurled downstream.
Sometimes you'll be swept away
Carried by forces
More powerful than you.
Keep your head above water
And go with the flow.
Listen to the RiverSpeak,
You'll be surprised
By a warm wind massaging your face.

32

Island

Island in the river,
Embraced by the tumbling waters.
River rock randomly placed
Along undisturbed banks.
Abundant plant life
Covers the oasis
In a blanket of greens.
Trees stand tall, well fed
At the island's center.
Earth nurtured by river
Year in and year out.

At the up river end
River somersaults
Over small boulders
And then splits in two.
River is an acrobat
Performing for the fish and birds.
No circus act rivals river's
Flexibility, dexterity
Equilibrium, concentration.
Tumbling waters,
Embracing island in the river.

33

Water in Motion

River is water,
Water in motion.
Falling water,
Falling fast,
Falling slow.
River is water in motion.
Water carving a
Serpentine path,
DNA spiral, S-curves,
The path of least resistance.
Water in motion,
Falling, dancing
Faster, slower, swirling
Toward the sea.
A powerful softness,
Pliable yet willful.
No stopping water in motion.
River swimming playfully
Through the center of the earth.
Splashing stroke by stroke,
Reaching without rushing,
Undulating water in motion.

34

Gentle River

The snows have melted mostly;
Now river flows more slowly.
There's gentleness
In the river
Under the hot sun.
The current is less threatening,
Inviting river worshippers
To wade into the coolness,
A baptismal rebirth.
An afternoon wind tickles,
As silence surrounds the rustling
Leaves in the treetops.
The wavelets splash
Soft against the bank;
Birds celebrate the coming of summer.
The solitude fills
With the presence.
Hunger's fire burns cool
In a blue glowing light.

35

River Stillness

A stillness in the river
After the spring run off.
The waters meander;
There's no hurry.
Taking time to enjoy
The journey to the sea.
Hearing and seeing
So much more
When walking
Rather than running.
River becomes aware
Of its natural life force.
It slows to inhale
The flowers,
Colored lights
Bud and blossom,
Inviting birds and humans
To stop rushing,
For what?
Another shopping bag
Of mall trash.
Drink river's stillness,
Strolling along the bank.

36

River and Sun

River meets sun,
Water and fire mingling
At the crack of dawn.
Steamy colors spread
Across the eastern horizon.
Usually water puts out fire.
Today river gives birth
To the morning light.
Sun penetrates
The dark night waters,
Illuminating polished
River rock, a golden treasure,
And warming the cool waters.
Birds chirp a song
About river and sun.
River falls – gravitation.
Sun rises – levitation.
Natural forces counteracting.
The sun is a golden treasure
Warming the cool galactic waters.
Water and fire mingling.

37

Master Sculptor

River is a master sculptor;
Rapid hands pouring over granite.
Another century or two
And the splash of boulders
Will take the shape
Of river's smooth flow
And rounded bubbling current.

What's time to a river?
There's no clock to punch,
No deadlines to make.
There's the seasons,
Sun and moon,
Day and night.
Forces, like strong fingers,
Squeeze, press, ply
Granules of granite
Into powerful, delicate shapes.
It's a work in progress
Displayed in nature's gallery.
The master sculptor's
Continuous creation;
Keeps the heart beating
As rapid hands pour over granite.

38
Embracing the Hardness with Softness

People come down to the river
Because they feel better.
Somehow river transmits
Energy through the air
Into the body, into the soul.
It feels good,
Peaceful, calm, soothing;
River carries away your troubles,
For the time being.
If you listen to RiverSpeak
You will find out
How to overcome your despair.
Then you'll feel better,
When you're away from river.

Banging your head against the wall
You refuse to change.
I've never seen a river
Bang its head against a wall.
River flows around a boulder
Embracing the hardness with softness.
Put that into continual practice
And river will be
Your constant companion.

39

The Sound of Falling Water

Enjoying the sound of falling water,
Falling water over river rock.
The morning sun dances
Through the rapids.
Gravity is friendly
At this small waterfall.
The sound, easy on the ears,
Centers in the alpha waves.
You can listen to this melody
Play over and over and over.
Before the first heart or drum
There was the sound of falling water.
Before the first hum or whistle
There was the sound of falling water.
Before the first grunt or groan
There was the sound of falling water.
The church bell rings nine
While the train whistles through town.
After that there's still
The sound of falling water.

40

Landscape Painting

There's a smooth flow
At this point on the river.
It invites a passersby
To contemplate
The gentle current.
It's Sunday morning,
Early in summer, mid-July.
The only creatures stirring
Are birds singing
At river's edge.
The sky,
Clear to the horizons.
The winds breathe,
And occasionally there's a soft sway
In the tree tops,
A reminder
That it's not an idyllic
Landscape painting.

41

Least Resistance

River meets resistance
Like a martial arts master;
It wears down an adversary
By offering minimal resistance.
It carves a canyon
Grain by grain.

Remember river
Whenever times are tough
Ask yourself,
How would river
Handle the problem?
River doesn't whine or bitch;
River doesn't complain or blame.
River offers minimal resistance.
Why bang your head against a wall
When you can carve a canyon
Grain by grain?
Why attack an obstacle
Head on?
Using your head,
You remember to offer
Minimal resistance.
Water flows around a rock
Not through a rock.

42

River In My Ears

River flows rapidly through my ears,
Washing my skin with sound.
Clinging and clutching,
Thoughts and feelings are swept
Into the cosmic sea.
Before I was more like rock,
Now I'm more like water.
River flows rapidly through my ears;
It's soothing sound,
Both soft and energizing,
Quiets me inside.
The silence is more powerful
Than thunder and lightning
Rocking the summer evening sky.
I'm peaceful in the
Center of the storm.
Listening to the river
Flowing rapidly through my ears
Has opened my eyes.

43

Blossoming into Light

The mountain snows have melted;
River has less to carry now.
The water level is low
On this stretch of the river.
Hundreds of river rocks
Are no longer under water.
A beautiful rock garden
Has blossomed into light.
You can hear them singing
Joyous notes of celebration.
Another year has passed
Standing firm beneath
The river.
"We no longer hold our breath
Watching the fish swim.
We soak up the summer heat
In order to stay warm
Throughout the winter.
Birds visit us
Telling stories of worlds
Upstream and down.
We have blossomed into light."

44

Soothing

Moving water, soothing,
Ripples shimmering in the morning light.
There are no speed limit signs;
The current goes as fast as it needs to go.
Dancing ripples from bank to bank.
Rhythmic current from mountain to sea.
River is natural in all ways
Centered in what it needs to do.
It doesn't look beyond its banks
For something else or someone else.
Moving water, soothing.
River's message clear,
Rhythmic motion up and down
Undulating current day and night.
Wavelets spreading forever
In liquid peaks and valleys.
Without uttering a word
River says it all.
Moving water, soothing
Ripples shimmering in morning light.

45
On the Edge of Summer

The fire
Has evaporated from river.
A stiff chill shivers
In the trees, in the current.
Clouds reflect
In the moving waters
Grey-green.
The end of a season
The beginning of another.
It starts to rain.
Tiny droplets high dive
From 2,000 foot clouds.
Passing a gliding hawk
Scanning the river bank
For a field mouse.
Joining the river,
Rain rides the rapids,
Hopping, skipping, jumping
From boulder to rock.
On the edge of summer
Embracing the fall.

46

Resonating with River

A breath of fresh air
Fills my lungs.
Effortless motion,
Resonating with river.
I glide whatever
Way I want to go.
There is no down or upstream.
River is always in motion,
And now, for a time, so am I.
The eye of the hurricane,
The zone, peak performance,
In rhythm with the planet's pulse.
Earth in the galactic river,
Whirling forever in orbit
Within greater and greater orbits,
Spilling over the Minnehaha
Falls of the universe.
A breath of fresh air
Fills my lungs,
Effortless motion
Resonating with river.

47

River Night

Night by the river
Dreaming, I'm awake.
I see continual water
Ever flowing, ever awake.
People sleep near river
Listening to the flow
Soothing the soul,
Night by the river.
Music rises from cafes,
Coffee houses and car radios
Like invisible smoke
Swirling and spiraling,
Sounds play in deep dreams.
River listens to itself,
Music to its own ears;
Never sleeping, never dreaming.
Night by the river
Dreaming, I am awake.
Tuning to the sound
Of moving river,
The music of the spheres
Passing through town
In the middle of the night.

48

Listening to River - Live

I'm back in the same spot
I've never been before.
The river sounds like it
Always has.
Yet, I'm hearing it like I
Never have.
My listening moves into the river
Hearing every drop
Falling and crashing
Into every other drop.
I don't know why
But when I listen to RiverSpeak
I feel uplifted, rejuvenated.
When I'm tired I feel energized,
When I'm rushed, I feel like
Slowing down.
When I'm lonely, I feel river
Is always with me and near me,
Even when I'm not physically present.
Listening to river – live;
It sounds like it always and
Never has
In the same spot
I've never been before.

49

Gravitation

River flows downhill.
Water seen, gravity unseen.
Gravity, an invisible, inaudible force.
Water is visible and audible.
River, in a way, makes
The unseen visible
And the unheard audible.
Gravity moves in waves,
In currents, in eddies,
In swirls, in vortexes,
In splashes, in peaks
And valleys.
Gravity sounds like a cosmic
Waterfall
Plummeting from above to below.
It's the universe applauding
Itself.
The sound of a million
Hands clapping,
The sound of silence,
The sound of one hand clapping.
The unseen, seen
The unheard, heard.

50
Alive with River

I've been to the river
Thousand of times,
No, a thousand, thousand times.
Now river is in my blood;
River is my blood.
My body alive with river;
My mind knows what river knows,
The understanding, the wisdom, the compassion
Bursting like whitewater,
Plunging from higher to lower.
I carry river everywhere I go;
I'm a human river flowing toward
The cosmic sea.
An undulating, twisting and turning;
A squiggle in the multidimensional pressure.
I've been to the river,
I've seen the sight.
I've heard the sound.
I'm alive with river,
A waterfall of life force.

51

River on the Other Side of River

The autumn evening sun
Lights up the cascading water
In brilliant geysers.
It's like looking
Into the noonday sun.
Eyes squinting,
Turning away for a moment
To avoid staring
Into the blinding white water.
The river plunges, bursting
On to the rocks and boulders.
Great white fans of water spread
Like minute transparent wings
Lifting the spirit of the river
On the other side of river.
Sprites and faeries play
In the cool, wet boil.
Imagination soars
Like Peter Pan through
Never, never land
Then skips laughing
Across the white water.

52

Dying Isn't So Bad

Bundled up in layers
My hands are cold.
Shivering, standing by river,
The warmth of Indian summer
Has set for another year.
The cool refreshing, rushing waters
Are icy now, cracking muscle and bone.
The sun enters Scorpio,
The sting of death.
River carries the poison
Through the heart, to the soul.
There's no antidote;
I wouldn't take one
If they had one.
Dying isn't so bad.
I'm getting used to it.
What's all the fuss about,
Worrying about the end?
It's the beginning in disguise,
It's birth from another point of view
Piercing the muscle and bone,
I bundled up.

53

Swept Downstream

Warm noon,
Cool river water.
The current is raw power,
Cascading and plunging.
I marvel at its naked force.
Comparing what I do
With what it's doing
I am humbled once again.
Before I sat down beside river
I was full of myself.
In just a few minutes
My "I" has been swept downstream.
The stresses, the strains
Doing too much in too short a time
Has been replaced by repose,
Emotional calm and peace of mind.
I've forgotten, for now,
What I have to do.
I feel the warm afternoon sun
And river's raw power.
Now I don't have to do anything,
Ahhh ... What a relief!

54

Mental Icicles Melting

I've been away from river;
I miss the powerful flow.
The winter cold
Has formed icicles in my mind,
Frozen thoughts of Christmas shopping
And New Year's resolutions.
I'm the only one here;
Every one else is inside
Trying to stay warm and fuzzy.
Taking a deep breath,
I feel the river flow
Through my soul.
The mental ice jam breaks free
From the winter of my mind.
Mental icicles melt;
There's an inner fire
Dancing with river water.
My feet are firmly planted
On the earthy bank.
I've invested my breathing
In myself – inhale, exhale;
I've been away too long.

55
January 1, 2001

Well, here we are – again,
Another day, another year.
Time, gravity and river
Like clockwork – tick, tock.
Unmechanical quantum mechanics.
Predictable, reliable, fluid,
A triad of triumphant forces.
Listening to the current
I hear the earth's pulse beat,
Seven beats per minute.
The earth is in great shape
Running the ultra, ultra, ultra
Marathon of all marathons;
Hurling through space-time
Like a leaf jetting downstream
In a whirlpool of gravity.
It's January 1, 2001; Happy New Year!
I'm sitting in the warm winter sun
Listening to river, the earth's heartbeat,
The sound of 2001 hands clapping.
It's a perpetual standing ovation.

56

Focusing on the Side Stream

Winter has lifted for an afternoon,
A touch of spring in February.
The river waters are icy
Despite the warm sun.
Here by river's edge
There's a trickle flowing,
A kind of mini-river,
A micro tributary
With a gentle current
Unlike the mighty torrent
Rushing like commuter traffic
In the main stream.
I like it here on the edge;
It slows my pulse
To focus on the side stream.
I see so much more.
The ripples are transparent,
The pebbles are softer
And easier to touch.
When spring comes
And the snows melt
The side stream will be
Part of the main stream again.

57

River's Magnetic Force

It's spring in early February,
A gift from old man winter,
For a day or two or three.
It's Sunday afternoon
And it seems everybody
Is by the river.
Some are dressed for summer
Wearing short sleeves and shorts.
One guy isn't even wearing a shirt.
The river is a kind of super magnet,
An electromagnet with water
Running through it
Instead of electricity.
No one can resist its pull;
There's something subtle
In the brain–body that's attracted
To river's invisible magnet force.
You can feel it,
But you really can't explain it.
You can't put your finger on it
But you know it's there.
There's a lot more to river
Than meets the eye.

58

Exceeding the Water Barrier

River, sun, flute,
Playing with the rushing waters.
Dancing waves rising-falling,
Calling to the unspoken within.
My mind spins to river
Through river, with river.
The beat of the rising-falling
Waves of cascading water.
Warm − air − still;
River − water − moving,
Moving at the speed of water,
Exceeding the water barrier.
Dancing with feelings and images,
Playing with rushing thoughts.
Hearing my name in silence,
Spinning in a whirl of flute.
I put my feet in the icy waters,
High Sierra snow this morning.
A shiver up my spine.
River − sun − flute.
Warm − air − still,
Exceeding the water barrier.

59
Playing in the Plunge and Tumble

River rushing from ice and snow
To steam, evaporating into thin air.
Leisure moments;
Water in slow motion,
Filling a river bed in spring.
Coming to a drop off
Water plunges
Into a free falling tumble
Over stones, rocks and boulders.
Cascading water has power;
A waterfall has real power.
I feel the leap of faith.
Water fearless,
No doubt,
Invading its mindful motion.
After a lifetime of meditation
Fear and doubt still stop the flow.
My ice cap melts more rapidly now.
Sometimes a part of me evaporates
When I take a deep breath.
I'm not anticipating the fall
As much as I used to do.
I play in the plunge and tumble
Where water and air merge.
Faithful, fearless,
Without a doubt.

60
And There's the River

There's the river
And there's *the* river.
I used to stand beside the river
And not see or hear the river.
I would look all around me;
I'd be standing in cold water
And ask passers by,
"Where is the river?"
Some would answer, "I don't know."
Others would answer,
"What are you deaf and blind?
You're standing up to your
Ankles in river."
I'd reply, "I am!"
One day I stopped looking,
I got real quiet inside;
I could hear myself think.
I stopped asking and thinking.
Suddenly, my feet were cold
And very wet, I was aware
River was all around me
And there's *the* river.

61

Rushing Coolness

Bathing in life river,
Soaking in the water
Like a psychic sponge.
The pores of my aura
Enjoying the rushing coolness.
It seems I never get my fill
Of that vital feeling.
At a certain point fullness
Is not really full
But a steady living presence
Gently rhythmic,
Softly breathing.
The forever rising and falling
Of river rapids
Tune me into life's pulse.
In–out, expand–contract
Gently breathing, softly rhythmic
Beating, beating, beating,
A place of motionless movement
Neither doing nor not doing
There, fullness is not really full,
Rather effortless breathing,
Enjoying the rushing coolness.

62

Imagine

Imagine never thinking;
No past, present, future.
Now is not a concept.
Now is just now;
There's no knowing of now.
River never thinks.
River is now.
River is timeless yet timeful.
Being close to river
Feel river from inside out.
Resonating vibration
Feeling deeply, soul connection.
River has no time to lose or gain
River knows no difference
From itself and anything else.
Earth is more pliable
Fire is less hot
Air is more soothing
Time pops like a white water bubble.
Imagine you are a river
A deep soul connection.

63

Spring

Spring along the river,
Green explosion.
There's something urgent
In the cool rapids.
The rushing water
Was snow only hours ago.
The ducks, the geese, the starlings
Flutter and fly and play
In and around the mighty current.
Spring along the river
Is about new energy.
A surge of life force
Pipping the shell of winter.
Melting the frozen water power.
Last year at this time
I was listening to the spring run off;
It still sounds like a continuous
Standing ovation.
Another spring stands up
And applauds;
Spring along the river.

64

River Sings

A stretch of river,
Quiet and meandering.
City is nowhere to be found.
Trickling waters sing
Birds join in the chorus.
A distant train whistle
Pierces the melody.
Soaking in the alpha waves
Resonating aura entrained;
Beta waves dissipate.
The river of my mind
The river I see and hear,
Now there's nothing I have to do
Hearing myself think,
I ask myself,
"Why don't I come
To this place more often?"
The question passes,
That's the answer.
The river of my mind
Is the river I see and hear.
This stretch of river sings.

65

Hot

It's so hot today
I came down to river
To cool off.
It's the hottest May
I can remember.
The occasional breeze
Relieves the heat stress.
Inhaling cool mountain water
Takes away the strain
Of heavy breathing.
The sweat trickles
Down wrinkles
Even as the river trickles
Over and around river rock.
Ah ... ah the breeze.
The cool water moving
Flowing ah – the breeze,
Nature's air conditioning
Without electricity
Without wires
Without cost – priceless
Hot – cool –
Ah the breeze.

66

Dancing on Moving Water

Transparent blue sky,
Golden green leaves
Sun dancing on moving water.
Duck, duckling jetting upstream.
A trout fisherman casting.
The wind still.
Peaceful thoughts
Meander through my mind.
Time slows
And stands still.
Fixed yet fluid,
A living photograph,
A memory in the making.
River serenades
My snapshot moment.
Sun dancing on moving water
Develops a meandering image,
Blue, golden green.
The fisherman reels
In a brown trout
Dancing on moving water.

67

Coming Up For Air

Currents swirling downstream,
A dance of light and water,
Coming up for air.
A granite boulder pokes
Its head out of river
To see what it can see.
People and cars crossing a bridge,
Pigeons frolicking and bathing.
Several other boulders
Poking their heads
Out of the water.
A poet writing a poem
About what I'm seeing.
Blue sky pokadotted
With etheric white clouds.
Buildings on either bank,
A Century 12plex theater,
A Masonic Lodge,
Artists' lofts.
A willow twig
Swimming downstream
Has caught around my neck.
Concentric water rings
Next to my living
Concentric water rings necklace.

68

Sweet River

Sweet river,
I can smell its vitality.
Inhaling energy
I feel more alive.
My spirit soars to other worlds
Even as I sit next to river,
Listening to the symphony
Within the sounds of rushing water.
Those worlds are free
Of crazy glue attachments
Like image, things and money.
River is transformed
Into an omnipresent cosmic sea.
Wading into the transparent ocean
I feel vitality, energy,
Sweet life force flowing
Up through my feet and legs
Into my torso and bathing
My heart with symphonic love.
The violins, the horns, the drums,
The splash of falling water,
The crash of cymbals.

69

Thunderstorm

Summer thunderstorms,
Run offs surging down canyons
Fill the usually clean waters
With mud and silt and dirt.
The skies swirl
Black with storm.
Thunder reverberates,
Building tension between
Earth and sky and water.
River is dark lightning
Striking the shadows
Of trees, boulders and critters.
The storm has swallowed
The sun whole.
Rain pelts the earth;
Tiny pools of water mix with dirt.
Muddy streamlets cascade into river.
The brown waters turn jet black.
Burdened with a heavy load,
River's back begins to bend
But does not break.
Water is eternally flexible.

70

A Care Free Stroll

A clear blue sky, no wind
A Sunday morning stroll along river,
Not a care in the world.
No have to's, no want to's,
No better do this or that.
White water rapids
Cascading downstream
With no deadline, no plan.
Water is care free,
It does what it does naturally.
It ripples, cascades, tumbles,
Flows, falls, rushes,
Eddies, somersaults and dances.
Free as the wind, the sky and the sun,
Free as an eagle soaring,
Free as a trout swimming,
Free as a Sunday morning stroll
I and river are one.
Not a care in the world.
A stroll is care free,
Especially on Sunday morning along the river.

71

Waiting for a Poem

Relaxed, calm, receptive,
Waiting patiently for a poem.
River is a poem of poems,
Combinations and permutations
Bordering on infinite shores.
I'm waiting for just one poem.
All I need to do, not do
Is pay attention, listen and watch
Without expecting,
Without assuming,
Without wanting.
Surprise! Instant thought wave.
The trickle, the tumble,
The white water rumble.
The wet, the wild, forever humble.
Flowing without a grumble.
Soundless speech, wisdom teach.
The endless undulating reach
Playing in the salty sands
On a vivid cosmic sea beach.
What a surprise!

72

The Nothing Place

Golden river wind,
Bursting airstreams.
Surging waters rushing.
Cascading sunlight,
Cool as mountain water.
Gushing time molecules
Orbiting circular rivers
Through the galaxies
Falling into earth beds.
Radiant blinding light
Seeing all in shadows
Surging waters rushing
To the nothing place,
The blackest black,
The deepest serpent time
In an underwater cave,
Dark fear brave
Bursting into liquid flame
Dark eternal blue.
Flickering in the river wind
Surging waters rushing
Spiraling through the nothing place.

73

Sipping Ice Tea through a Yellow Straw

Hot summer evenings;
Sun falling into red.
River and wind cool my skin.
Eyes and muscles strain
From the heat, the heat
Hour after hour, endless heat.
Sipping ice tea through
A yellow straw.
A gust of wind dries
The sweat on the back
Of my neck.
The river invites me
Into its cool bubble bath.
Hot sun displays orange and pink.
I wade into the stream.
A surge of cool energy
Rises through my feet,
Up my legs and into my heart.
My eyes and muscles relax.
I see color and shapes
Where I saw nothing before.
Sipping ice tea
Through a yellow straw.

74

Dreams Come True

The sounds of surging
River dashing and splashing,
Currents cutting and slashing.
Feeling the intensity
Flowing through my body,
Resonating from river.
Blue imagination
Dotted with playful thoughts,
Gold and silver swirls
Eddy images, time rings.
Suddenly the rushing waters
Open into a looking glass,
Past – present – future – now.
Where you are is where
You need to be.
What you are is where
You've been up to now.
Now is the start
Of where you will be.
Be totally present
And your future will
Be dreams come true.

75

Respect for River

The force of falling water
Punches you in the guts.
Bam, it knocks you off your feet.
And this waterfall
Is only three,
Maybe four feet high.
Crashing, pounding, striking
Great boulders with the force
Of 10,000 jack hammers.
When I take my warm cozy bath
I'll have a lot more respect
For the power in falling water.
The dark, green, brown river explodes
Into psychotic white water.
Billions of bursting bubbles
Create an exhilarating fall out.
Craggy boulders are warn
Smooth as new born skin.
Tiny electric light fingers
Point toward a heavenly dome
Then makes a fist full of water
Punching downstream in cascades
Of mighty falling water.

76
Roaring Laughter

Shimmering sunlight
On moving water.
Light and water merging
Then falling, plunging, roaring.
A waterfall generating power.
An energizing, uplifting force
Wraps the aura in vivid awareness.
Absorbing the whitewater show,
Drinking the dynamic flow
With wide open eyes and ears.
The sparkling, twinkling, dancing
Water-light, fearless, takes flight.
Free falling a second or two
Then roaring laughter.
There's no volume control;
Continual laughing until crying.
Tears cascading down weathered cheeks.
The belly hurts, gasping for air.
Sudden silence
Within the river roar.
A deafening divine silence
Reveals shimmering sunlight
On moving water.

77

River Feeding Frenzy

River duck, river geese,
Fishing for dinner.
Geese grooming,
Waiting for dinner to float by.
A bag lady throws breadcrumbs.
A goose stops grooming and feeds.
Writing this poem twelve ducks,
No thirteen, no fourteen
Congregate
Watching me writing this poem.
Waiting for food from me
Six or seven swim downstream.
Dipping beaks under water
Nibbling at river morsels.
Quack, quack, quack, quack, quack,
Eating an evening river feast.
A starling finds two McFrench fries,
A delight this evening
On the riverbank.
Six ducks pass
Swimming up stream in formation.
A woman throws movie popcorn
From a bridge,
Feeding frenzy satisfied.

78

Breathing Holy Water

Breathing the energy of falling water,
Lungs filled with holy river.
Dark brown-green transformed
In a free fall of water bubbles.
Moving water, falling water, energy
Filling the air with holy river
With transparent clouds
Of rejuvenating life force.
Without being in the river
Bathing in the essence of river.
Water crashing against water,
Walls of water merging.
Molten, bubbling river
Jumping, leaping, dancing
A downstream dream.
Breathing holy liquid air,
Blood carried river,
Heart pumping presence.
Time stretches at high speed;
Mind-heart-spirit freed.
A waterfall dream comes true
After breathing holy river.

79
Rippled Moments

Rippled moments streaming,
River sounds dreaming;
Sitting alone yet not alone
Being one with the flowing water.
Seeing the rise and fall,
The fall and rise – wise rhythms
Upstream, downstream river ripples.
Not separate, not out there,
One within here, not out there,
Not in here, resonating with
The natural river frequency.
Beating hearts of planet earth,
Hundreds of hearts beating,
Drumming in rhythm with rivers.
Music of the here-now
Dreaming the present, in the presence.
Forever rising-falling water
Flowing through beating hearts.
Rippled moments bursting time,
Sitting alone, yet not alone,
Being one with flowing water
Rippled moments dreaming.

80

Goosebumps and Shivers

Cool, fall morning river,
Goosebumps and shivers.
Gentle current under
The Virginia Street Bridge.
On the shady side of river
Looking at the sunny side,
Seeing the shadow play
Of pigeons on cement walls.
Beneath the surface
Are moss covered rocks,
Small boulders,
An unopened glass bottle
And a pair of silver rimmed sunglasses.
Imagine plain dark glasses
Taking on the magic of river.
Maybe I'll fish them out
On the summer solstice,
Put them on and see invisible images.
A vision quest revealing river secrets
Like the 10,000 year history
Of this spot on the shady side of river,
Giving me goose bumps and shivers.

81

River Dreams

River dreams
Clouds of water.
Memories created;
Memories destroyed.
Dreams flowing into dreams,
Ride the wild waters.
White rapid thoughts
Speeding through silent minds.
Refreshing images,
Energizing waterfalls,
Supplying electricity
To wired souls
Floating in water clouds.
Sunlight glittering
On bubble walls
Dreams blowing by,
Feelings cascading
Over liquid rock.
Another river dream
Fading in a downstream sunset.
Memories rising,
Memories falling.

82

On Stone Lily Pads

Sitting on a boulder
On the edge of river.
Floating downstream
On a ton of rock,
A lily pad of stone
Carried into a levitation world,
Current feelings passing by.
Fall foliage free in the wind,
Spinning rock, cosmic traveler
Galaxy hopping from light to matter
From matter to light, star stuff.
Today's dream comes with a musical score.
The rise and fall of rustling leaves
Blowing crescendos in surround sound
Barely audible then building.
Bushes, small trees and big trees,
Leaves shaking in the breeze.
A natural jazz symphony,
Improvisational current feelings.
On the edge of river
Floating in a levitation world
On a stone lily pad.

83

Best Fall Dress

River has put on
Her best fall dress
Draped in gold, yellow and orange.
Sashaying downstream,
She feels more beautiful than ever.
You can't look her way
And not notice her colorful curves.
Ooooo-Weeeee, (wolf whistle).
She can wet my whistle any time.
I can't ask her
For a phone number
She doesn't have one.
She can't dress up like that
And not have someone
On her arm.
I put on my best suit
And step up close.
I can feel her curves.
I can whisper in her ear
"You're beautiful in that dress!"
Without saying a word
She takes my arm
And we dance downstream together.

84

Winter River

Water, cold as cracked glass
Broken solar reflections,
Fire flickering
Between the ripples,
The first day of winter river.
This year river is drinking
Its fill of high country snow,
Melting in the afternoon heat.
In some mysterious way
River has returned within,
Despite the perpetual motion.
Maybe the water spirits
Have hibernated in the caves
Inside giant river boulders,
Dreaming of sunshine
And warm crackling fires.
Sleeping winter river.
Movement is fire;
Stillness is ice,
Freezing, melting.
Fire flickering
Between the ripples,
River winter solstice.

85
Counting on River

I can count on river
Flowing to the sea
For a timeless eternity,
Spinning, whirling
Spiraling energy.
The force of water
Cutting and carving
In earth, through earth
Into the bowels of earth.
Water is soft,
Yet it cuts
Through rock hard granite.
The force of water
Puts out the force of fire.
River flows to the sea;
You can count on that.
Wet, wild mighty river
Crashes into giant waves,
Water against water,
An explosion of water.
The force of water squared.
I can count on river.

86

Winter River Dream

Whirlpool images,
Winter river dream
Downstream all night.
REM sleep,
Dream stories
Float and churn and plummet
Like titanic waterfalls
Dropping three or four thousand feet.
Vivid dreamscapes unfold,
Appear out of thin air.
Walking through time warps
River dream, River dream.
Phobias and fantasies
Revealed, exposed naked truths.
You can not hide in a dream,
River flows to the sea.
Whirlpool images
Spin my thoughts
Until milk turns into butter,
Spreading colorful scenes
Across my holographic mind.
Spring, right around the corner,
Beckoning my river dream to wake.

87

Spring Vitality

Solar kick ass power
Microwaves alpine snow.
The river rises
Like bread baking.
The first spring heat wave
Brings river to a rapid boil.
A brief mist
Appears and disappears.
A thin blanket of steam
Warms the winter chill.
River mysteriously pulling,
Drawing, propelling.
People, young and old,
Birds, ducks, geese and pigeons
Swept into a whirlpool
Of springtime vitality.
The bear hibernation ends;
The fresh smell of sweet water,
An overwhelming thirst
Shakes bear from a cozy cave,
Drinking, drinking, drinking
River vitality.

88

Fish Mother, Fish Son

Fish mother,
Fish son,
River spirit.
Secret fish swimming
Silent zigzagging.
Casting to the river's cadence.
What is the movement
On and under moving water?
Circling, turning, swimming
In the current
Through the current,
Cross current.
Worms and lures
Cold water, warm sun
Reeling in, spinning.
Casting, no fish, casting.
Fish love, fish eggs,
Baited hook, bite, hooked.
Reel in river trout
Splish-splash
On and under moving water.

89

Galloping River

Galloping cascades
River rising, falling
Stampeding waters
Running toward the sea.
A million liquid horsepower
Exploding from snowcapped peaks,
Blowing like the wind
Through gullies, canyons, valleys,
Nature's aqueducts,
Channeling river
To a cosmic destination,
A limitless sea.
Water forever,
No start, no finish
No in between
Water in motion.
Vast underwater rivers,
Jet streams giving free rides
To all who want to climb aboard
And hold on for dear life.
Galloping, stampeding,
A riptide of overpowering
Force, a million horsepower
Running through river
Like lightning.

90

River's Heart Is Always Open

I've spent more time
More energy
Getting to know this river
Than getting to know
Most people.
River's heart
Is always open.
Most human hearts
Have been slammed shut.
I never have to knock,
I don't have to find a key,
I don't have to unlock
Door after door after door.
River has no door to open.
River's heart is always open
24/7, 365 days a year,
Even on holidays.
My love for this river
Widens, deepens, expands.
My heart is more open
Than ever before
And I didn't have to waterfall in love.
River's heart is always open.

91

In the Roar, Silence

Wind, clouds, sun, water,
Trees, birds, man, woman,
All embracing river.
Bright lights, camera, action,
Hot skin, the glare.
Sunglasses soften the sun.
Cascading river roaring,
Perpetual roaring
Sometimes louder,
Sometimes softer.
A torrent, a trickle
A quiet mind tickle
I dive into the roar,
Cool skin silence
In the roar, silence.
The silence so loud,
Ear popping loud.
I thought only jet engines
And rock music
Could make you deaf.
Silence is deafening
In the roar, silence.

92

Riverscape

Perpetual moving riverscape
Never fixed, always flowing,
Dancing to the rhythm
Of ripples, waves and rapids.
Can I have this dance?
Listen to the water music,
Feel the beat, moving feet
Come dance with me.
Earth to water free
Skipping across currents.
Drowning is not an option.
Always flowing, dancing
Riverscape moving,
Strumming the ripples
Plucking the waves,
Improvising, creating
A dance that's never
Been danced before.
River jazz dancing
In a perpetual riverscape
Forever feeling the beat.

93

Repeating River

Sitting on a river rock
Where I've never sat before
Even though I've sat here
A thousand times before.
The same is always different
The familiar an illusion,
A secure feeling
But an illusion nonetheless.
The spring run off
Zooming from right to left,
Giving me a breath
Of fresh water.
Ionic breathing,
Revitalized blood flowing,
Pumping through the heart
Of ten thousand years
Of repeating river
Over and over again
Sounding the same
But never the same
Always different.
Sitting on a river rock
Where I've never sat before
Even though I've sat here
A thousand times before.

94

Red Oxygen, Blue Feeling

Just a touch of wind
Tickling tree top leaves.
Cold rushing water - spring.
Hot green tea cooling
Steam swirls rising,
Evaporating into mountain air.
Blood resonating with river,
Red oxygen, blue feeling.
I don't have to go anywhere
When I'm here - now.
Thoughts tickle my mind,
Feelings giggle my soul.
Laughing waters
From Minnehaha Creek
To Minnehaha Falls
To the mighty Mississippi,
The river of my childhood.
The rushing water in my veins.
Visiting the source.

95

A Poem Plays on Paper

I've only a few
River moments left.
Each one is forever,
Sitting in poetry meditation,
Listening to a word stream.
Inaudible at first,
A mumbo-jumbo noise.
Then out of sound chaos
Flows a clear current,
An audible sound stream
In English, it could be Spanish or ...
River is multilingual;
She invented language.
I feel a poem in my heart;
Words write themselves
Playfully on the paper.
This river moment
Is ink rushing
Through a sterling silver pen
Splashing on a made in China
Spiral notebook page.
A poetry prayer is answered
Playfully on the paper.

96
RiverBed

River bottom, riverbed
Sleeping, dreaming
Ever caressed by the current.
During draughts
Her earthen crust
Exposed to fire and moon
Cracks dry.
River bottom supports,
Embraces the perpetual motion.
Migrating south for the winter,
Water wings gliding
On spiral eddies
Coming in for a landing.
Birds and rivers know
How to gracefully land.
Riverbed made
In centuries
For millenniums.
River lies down
On a soft earth bed
Dreaming of water.

97

River High

Sitting next to river,
I've sat here so many times.
The connection, instantaneous.
Wow! Oh my God!
The energy, feeling,
A natural high,
A rushing water
Explosion of life force.
I'm calmer, more alive
Than I felt a few minutes
Before I sat next to river.
I'm bathed in an energy
That's so sweet,
So naturally invigorating
My mind skips
On white water rapids
Sending my consciousness
To a world wet
In soothing energy.
Better than a full
Body massage
Is Zen meditation river.

98

Splish Splashing

Falling water, falling water
Splish slash, splish splash
Falling water, falling water
Gravitational force
From above to below
Returning to the source,
Here, yet going there.
The river's constant flow
Splish splashing, splish splash,
Subtracting lower from higher
Equals river's energy.
The difference between
Positive and negative
Is gravity splish splashing.
Water falling, water falling,
Fearless plunging water
From up to down
In the center of town
From mountain peak
To sea level seek,
Gravity, water, river.

99

RiverSpeak Made Flesh

Coming and going,
River ever flowing.
I've gone to river
And left river
In terms of time and space.
In non-Newtonian now
I've never come and gone.
Thought – There – River.
Twelve men fishing on the Rogue.
Five fish caught in two days.
Archetypal message
Resonating DNA.
The cycle is complete
Renewing, repeating, recycling,
Merging with river energy,
RiverSpeak made flesh.
I and river are one,
A marriage made in heaven
The mystery of two
Fusing in the sun.
The circuit is complete
Alternating river current,
Coming and going.

100

RiverSpeaking

RiverSpeaking in water tones,
I hear myself flow.
Gravity is my mother,
The sun is my father
I give birth to myself
In the white water
In the melting snow
When rain touches me.
I hear myself flow,
My thoughts are splashes
My emotions are waterfalls
My heart is soft current
I have spoken – listen
I am speaking – listen
I hear myself flow
I am aware – I know
I see without eyes
I touch without hands
I hear without ears
RiverSpeak, RiverSpeak
I hear myself flow,
I am aware – I know.

About the Author

Greg Nielsen has been an author for over thirty years. His writing experience ranges from non-fiction, to fiction and includes poetry, magazine, film, television, radio and business writing. His books have sold more than a million copies worldwide and have been translated into many languages. In 1988 he started Conscious Books, publishing books for himself and other authors. He has traveled throughout the U.S. doing workshops, seminars, booksignings and media appearances. Some of his published works include *Pyramid Power, Pendulum Power, Beyond Pendulum Power, Tuning to the Spiritual Frequencies, Light Waves* (poetry) and *MetaBusiness*. His poem, "Red Oxygen, Blue Feeling" received honorable mention in the Davoren Hanna Poetry Competition, an international poetry contest based out of Eason's Bookshop in Ireland. Greg received the Evelyn Bridges Poetry award while attending Colorado College.

He can be reached by e-mail: greg.nielsen@charter.net

About the Cover Artist – Cyndee Chavez

Cyndee's high school art teacher recognized and encouraged her creativity. After high school she attended Brooks College in Los Angeles where she studied clothing design and merchandising. Later she enrolled at the University of Nevada studying Fine Art and Art History. There her artistic talents found expression in metal sculpture, found objects and oil paintings. Soon she began to show her work in the Reno/Tahoe area.

Cyndee now lives in the San Francisco Bay Area. Her studio overlooks a spectacular view of Carquinez Straits. She has completed her certification as a Graphic Artist. Her work includes logo and caricature design as well as identity packages and various graphics projects.

She can be reached by e-mail: bcreativedesign@mac.com.

CPSIA information can be obtained
at www.ICGtesting.com
Printed in the USA
FSHW010401130220
66940FS